Christian Laase

Drowning in e-mails – from a helper to a burden and ho
e-mail

I0013283

GRIN - Verlag für akademische Texte

Der GRIN Verlag mit Sitz in München hat sich seit der Gründung im Jahr 1998 auf die Veröffentlichung akademischer Texte spezialisiert.

Die Verlagswebseite www.grin.com ist für Studenten, Hochschullehrer und andere Akademiker die ideale Plattform, ihre Fachtexte, Studienarbeiten, Abschlussarbeiten oder Dissertationen einem breiten Publikum zu präsentieren.

Christian Laase

Drowning in e-mails — from a helper to a burden and how to get back to an efficient use of e-mail

GRIN Verlag

Bibliografische Information der Deutschen Nationalbibliothek: Die Deutsche Bibliothek verzeichnet diese Publikation in der Deutschen Nationalbibliografie; detaillierte bibliografische Daten sind im Internet über http://dnb.d-nb.de/ abrufbar.

1. Auflage 2005
Copyright © 2005 GRIN Verlag
http://www.grin.com/
Druck und Bindung: Books on Demand GmbH, Norderstedt Germany
ISBN 978-3-638-83166-6

EUROPEAN BUSINESS SCHOOL

International University Schloss Reichartshausen am Rhein

Seminar Paper

at the Department for Logistics and Business Engineering

Winter 2005 (Semester 7)

Drowning in e-mails – from a helper to a burden and how to get back to an efficient use of e-mail

Name:

Christian Maria Laase

Date:

30th of September 2005

Table of Contents

List of Figures

1.   Introduction

The significance of email as a modern medium for communication has grown fast and sustainable. The technical basis, especially the availability of a digital infrastructure enabled the global spread of email as a user friendly, flexible and versatile medium. By now email can be considered as one of the most frequently used applications of the internet. The advantages of email as being low in costs but high in speed and reliability led to its increasing use and significance. Furthermore its quality of being "viral" through easy forwarding and multi-receiver-sending has opened new possibilities for communication. On the one hand the disposability of email has led to these new trends, on the other hand the very same quality can be held responsible for the short-lived and unsustainable attributes of email.[1]

Since the emergence of the first communication through electronic mail the face of email concerning both quality and quantity has changed significantly. In terms of quality it has changed from a simple substitute for the hand written letter to today's most important tool for collaboration, knowledge-management, online marketing and global business communication. Furthermore it is "now used for multiple purposes: document delivery and archiving, work task delegation; and task tracking. It is also used for storing personal names and addresses, for sending reminders, asking for assistance, scheduling appointments, and for handling technical queries." Electronic mail can be considered as vital precursor for globalization and the modern information society.

Its commercial use for offers, contracts, orders etc. created demand for an obliging and explicit legal framework together with new standards regarding electronic signature, identification and data safety.

The trend of an increasing quantity of electronic mail is strongly related to its development, standardization and availability of digital infrastructure.

---

[1] See STEIN (2004), p. 1.

The exponentially increasing amount of email per day has led to serious problems regarding efficiency in the use of the medium and to new challenges both for the technical infrastructure, the software and the user.

1.1 Scope of the Work and Structure of the Seminar Paper

The topic of this paper is how the increasing amount of email traffic is affecting the efficient use of the medium negative and which strategies may be promising to find back to a pleasant and efficient use for personal and business related communication. The scope of the work is to give a general overview of emerging problems, of the different components of the increasing email traffic and possible solutions to encounter the problems.

After a general introduction in chapter one, chapter two focuses on the emerging problems related to increasing mail traffic. The different areas in which problems occur are introduced separately. Chapter three and four describe the two main components of the increasing traffic, relevant private and business related correspondence on the one side and spam email on the other side. Strategies how to cope with the increasing mail volume are given for each problem. Chapter four introduces different spam filters and a legal framework to encounter spam. Chapter five gives a short conclusion of the paper. The paper ends with the listing of all references.

2.   Problems resulting from increasing Email Traffic

The data volume generated by electronic mail has been growing constantly since the beginning of digital communication. Even though "advantages over other technologies such as the telephone, and even face-to-face interacting"[2] are pointed out by users, its trend of an exponential growth through out the years has led to the emergence of serious problems due to limitations of the related resources. The problems can be split up into three different main areas:

- technical limitations such as memory and bandwidth
- monetary limitations due to increasing needs for technical equipment and human labor for administering the incoming and outgoing data
- personal limitations such as decreasing trust and willingness to use the medium

All these consequences cause higher costs for all participating parties. Important IT-Resources are blocked, the effective and efficient use of email is prevented and the productivity of the user is lowered.

2.1   Technical Problems

Negative effects through spam appear in all areas where technical infrastructure is involved. Especially ISPs which are running the mail servers are strongly affected by the increasing data volume and higher costs.

According to an IDC study, the number of email per day will grow from 5 billion in 1999 to estimated 60 billion in 2006.[3] With an average data volume of 59 KB/mail, the daily data volume has grown up to 1.829 Terabyte per day, loading the global mail server infrastructure with 3.35 Petabyte per year, according to Forrester Research.[4]

---

[2] See SIDNER AND WHITTAKER (1996), p. 2.
[3] See IDC (NO YEAR).
[4] See FORRESTER RESEARCH (2002).

The performance of the whole internet is stressed. To cope with these high data volumes, ISPs have to invest capital which is, in the end, paid by the user and the customer community.

2.2   Economical Problems

On the one hand „email has contributed to the growth of distributed organizations, by allowing people in different geographical areas to communicate across time and space."[5] Since the spread of email for business related communication email has increased efficiency and led to economical growth.

By today, employees spend high amounts of their work time using email for variable tasks. Employees suffer from the increasing volume of email in their inbox. The over all efficiency is affected negative. Results are additional costs for economy and public.

By the year 2000, 43% of all incoming mail in a professional environment was not business related.[6] Additional costs companies around the world will have to invest in 2003 in terms of additional server infrastructure to manage the high data volume are estimated $20,500,000,000.[7] A company with 10,000 email users without anti-spam protection will loose 49$ per year per mailbox due to decreasing efficiency of the employees.[8]

Other related problems for the companies can emerge in terms of workflow due to email and important information being overlooked or lost by the employees, "outstanding tasks, partially read documents and conversational threads"[9]. In a long term prospective the use of email as a reliable medium for global communication can loose its credibility.

2.3   Personal Problems

As well on a personal level the individual user is affected negative by spam. The emergence of spam has led to significant change in the relationship of the users to the internet and how they evaluate the internet. Even the users' behavior has been affected.

---

[5] See SIDNER AND WHITTAKER (1996), p. 1.
[6] See RAY, THOMAS AND DARREN (NO YEAR), p. 2.
[7] See EPRIVACY GROUP (2003), p. 1.
[8] See EPRIVACY GROUP (2003), p. 1.
[9] See SIDNER AND WHITTAKER (1996), p. 1.

Common effects are that users use email less because of spam, they loose trust in the medium. Common fears are that important mail is being overlooked or children are affected negative by the offensive content of spam.[10]

According to Pew Internet & American Life Project, 25% of the users say the ever increasing volume of spam has reduced their overall use of email[11]; 70% of email users say spam has made being online unpleasant or annoying. Only 14% say spam is no problem at all.[12]

In general the perceived negative effects by the users are of higher gravity concerning their personal email accounts compared to their work email accounts. Even though the overall number of received email is higher in the work email account, the relative percentage of spam is higher in the personal email account. Many work email accounts are pre-filtered by the companies IT-infrastructure.[13]

---

[10] See FELLOWS (2003), p. 29.
[11] See FELLOWS (2003), p. I.
[12] See FELLOWS (2003), p. II.
[13] See FELLOWS (2003), p. 38.

3.   Personal and Business related Email

The increasing volume of email traffic consists of two different kinds of communication. Besides high numbers of spam and junk mail an increasing number of valuable and meaningful email correspondence concerning personal and business related topics can be hold responsible. The increasing usage of email in almost all areas of daily life led to a displacement of classical forms of communication and to new challenges for the user. High numbers of relevant email in the inbox make it more difficult for the user to make efficient use of the medium and to manage their communication.

Emerging problems are the inability to respond quickly to important email due to a constant stream of new communication, tasks etc. throughout the day. The user is more likely to loose track of his correspondence, loosing sight of important items in his inbox or simply overlook urgent email. The overwhelming volume of incoming email leads to a vicious circle of in-responsiveness and the attempt to catch up.

Changing purposes of email communication such as document delivery, archiving, work task delegation and knowledge management led to changing needs in administering, archiving and storing data. Lucidity of all stored data and the ability to find and access important information is getting more complex and time consuming to handle. Email is vital part of almost all business areas such as Accounting, Sales, Human Resources and medium for sensitive data and contracts. The user has to take theses new requirements into consideration, especially legal aspects in a professional environment have gained importance.

Additionally long-term email correspondence and correspondence with a high number of participating senders and receivers requests new approaches in administering contacts and contact data.[14]

Besides new software models for email clients such as conversational threads and graphical display of complex correspondence[15], new holistic approaches for integrating email successful into the whole business process haven been developed.

---

[14] See WHITTAKER, JONES AND TERVEEN (2002), p. 1.

3.1 Email Lifecycle Management

The following paragraph is based on the IQ-solutions whitepaper "Email Lifecycle Management".[16]

To keep pace with new trends for email correspondence and to guarantee an efficient use of the medium for the company, new solutions for an extensive integration of all electronic communication into the complete work flow and through the whole lifecycle of the email have been developed recently. Email Lifecycle Management is such an integrated and holistic approach to comprehend, classify, process and track email including attachments, graphics and groupware discussions throughout the whole business process.

ELM can be used to generate competitive advantages through higher efficiency in email use and to relate email applications automatically to company specific regulations and specifications. Especially the compliance with all legal aspects e.g. the duty of storing business related communication and assuring safety of sensitive internal or customer data has to be assured. Additionally improvements of business processes through automatic connection to database systems can be realized. Besides lower costs and a better organization ELM provides a higher productivity and efficiency in a dynamic business environment through supporting decision processes.

3.2 ELM Process

The lifecycle of an email consists of seven strongly related processes. Every process is based on company-, department- or user specific regulations. Compliance regarding all different processes has to be guaranteed throughout the lifecycle.

---

[15] See IBM (2003).
[16] See GROUP TECHNOLOGIES (2005).

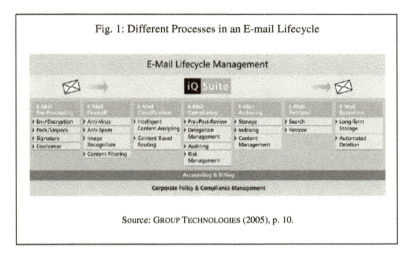

Fig. 1: Different Processes in an E-mail Lifecycle

E-Mail Lifecycle Management

Source: GROUP TECHNOLOGIES (2005), p. 10.

Pre-Processing: Pre-Processing ensures that all incoming mail is automatically decrypted and uncompressed before filtering. Outgoing mail is being encrypted and compressed, legal disclaimers and signatures are added. This first step is vital for good organization and high efficiency. Company regulations are more consistently followed and danger of legal problems is minimized.

Firewall: According to variable settings, all email traffic is checked for viruses, spam and other unwanted content. Multiple filter and techniques for recognizing viruses and spam can be used. A detailed protocol of all process steps allows a continuous and up to date view over the whole email traffic. Pre-selection of unwanted email can increase efficiency of the employees, enhance corporate image and customer satisfaction.

Classification: Automatic classification of email is an important tool for improving business processes. Content of incoming email is analyzed, categorized and can be send to different receivers within the company. Content classification also offers the possibility to automatically generate key words and context specific indices for effective archiving.

Compliance: Compliance is on of the most important factors regarding a safe email correspondence. Compliance means the conformance with all public laws, legal and internal regulations. To fulfill all these regulations automatically, semantic context identification is used. If certain information such as financial statements or customer data is not free for external communication via email, it can be detected automatically and stored in a special database for further investigation.

Archiving: To fulfill all legal requirements email can be archived automatically or through an archiving solution from a third party. The classification and archiving can be operated through different settings. Email will be stored in its original state and with all key words and indexations.

Retrieval: The possibility to retrieve or track back all email is an important part of the archiving process. Users need the possibility to easily search and find all relevant correspondence easy and fast.

Retention: Another part of the archiving and retrieval process is the long term storage in third party database systems. Retention of all stored email can be controlled automatically. Through complex content filter all relevant information can be stored and irrelevant data can be deleted automatically. All internal and external correspondence can be stored on groupware servers.

ELM is used throughout all seven steps of an email lifecycle. Automatic connection to related systems such as archives, CRM and ERP solutions is possible. Compliance with laws and legal regulations is assured in every phase. ELM provides potential for a safe, holistic and efficient use of email correspondence and helps to cope with the increasing flood of email correspondence in every part of the business process.

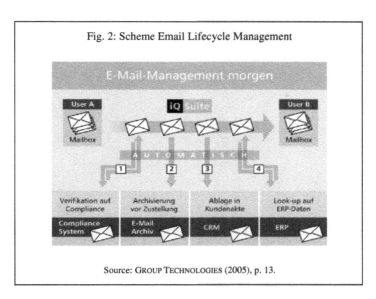

Fig. 2: Scheme Email Lifecycle Management

Source: GROUP TECHNOLOGIES (2005), p. 13.

4.   Unsolicited commercial Messages: SPAM

Besides the increasing number of personal or business related email, spam can be considered as the biggest thread for the user today. Unsolicited commercial message, or spam, is a term which describes email by an unknown sender send to your inbox. It's the electronic version of the classical junk mail.

The content of spam can be almost every topic; generally it's a commercial advertisement, a hoax or a worm. Classical and almost famous content of spam are pornography, online pharmacies, the "Nigerian connection" and other ´get rich quick´ schemes.

By today spam represents estimated 2/3 of all email traffic[17] and has grown from a simple direct mail advertisement to a serious thread for digital infrastructure, technical resources, users and economy. Spam is undermining the integrity of the internet and email.[18]

Fig. 3: Content of received Email

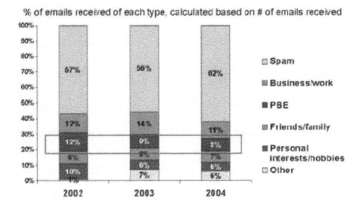

Source: DOUBLECLICK (2004), P. 2.

---

[17] See DoubleClick (2004), p. 2.
[18] See FELLOWS (2003), p. I.

4.1   Spam Filter

Spam filters are used to block spam email from being delivered to the user's mailbox. Since the emergence of spam as a serious thread a remarkable development of all kinds of anti-spam solutions has started.

Yahoo directory listed 61 different commercial companies offering Anti-spam and Anti-junk mail software solutions.[19] Anti-spam software has grown to an important economical factor for the software industry.

There are two different approaches in filtering spam: central filter are run on the mail server of the ISP, while local filter are run on the user platform or on the companies IT architecture. The central filter offers advantages through a decreasing traffic and use of bandwidth and memory of the ISP servers while problems with the definition of spam for the ISP and the user may occur. The local solution enables the user to set all settings by own preferences but has no positive effects on the performance of the whole internet.

By today, there is no perfect filter for recognizing spam absolutely safe. Occurring problems are "false negative", spam that reaches the mailbox, and more important "false positive", important email that does not reach the mailbox of the user because it is classified as spam by accident. The last problem leads to decreasing trust of the user in the medium and can be held responsible for serious consequences for business and economy. Problems with filtering spam are due to the dynamic nature of spam which requires the development of adaptive spam filter and the combination of different filter methods.

Methods for filtering spam reliable will gain importance for the efficient use of email. Due to the fact that business and personal correspondence as well as spam will increase in the future, users have to become more conscious about their email. The fact that the number of spam is increasing with the relatively highest rate, a successful approach to control spam will be inevitable. A right mixture of technological approaches such as

---

[19] See YAHOO (2005)

spam filter, legal aspects such as an explicit legal framework as well as the responsible use of email by the users has the potential for a promising solution.

In the following paragraph, classical techniques for filtering spam and new approaches for encountering the problem will be introduced.

4.1.1 Classical Filter Methods

As long as not referred separately, the following chapter is based on the Spam Datasheet by BlackSpider Technologies.[20]

Black lists: These are operated by commercial organizations or communities of interested users on a collaborative basis. In blacklists IP addresses of machines that have been sending spam are collected. Local as well as central spam filter can access these databases in real time and block incoming spam.

Well known blacklist are MAPS, spam Prevention Early Warning System (SPEWS), and the Open Relay Database (ORDB).[21]

White lists: The inverse of a blacklist where only mail from a known sender is accepted. All email from unknown senders is being blocked and forwarded to a special low-priority folder. This technique brings the problem of high numbers in "false positive" email. Therefore a white list is not a typical spam filter but more a "trusted seal" for email.[22]

Even though white lists are 100% effective in blocking unwanted spam, two major problems occur. Additional efforts have to be done by the user to set up his white list and keep it up to date. If there is a high number of spam in the low-priority folder, it is difficult and time consuming to identify relevant email.[23]

---

[20] See BLACKSPIDER TECHNOLOGIES (2004).
[21] See ARRISON (2004), p. 15.
[22] See ARRISON (2004), p. 15.
[23] See GOLBECK AND HENDLER (2004), p. 1.

Lexical Analysis: Based on a dynamic list of key words and phrases, a detailed lexical analysis of the entire email is being conducted including message envelope, headers, subjects and body text.

Collaborative Spam Database: Several spam databases such as Vipul's Razor exist on the internet. They work like Blacklists on a collaborative basis. Unlike Black lists, individual internet users submit spam mails and every mail is given a unique signature. Spam filters can access these databases and use the data for identifying potential spam.

Bayesian Filtering: In a Bayesian filter, two different databases for email are created. One consists of spam and the other one of valid email. All data in the databases is being 'tokenized' and a comparative analysis of the frequency of the different tokens in the two databases is conducted. Based on the analysis the method can identify spam by the probability certain tokens appear in an email.

Spam Traps: Comparable to 'honey pots' that can be used to catch bees, spam traps are email accounts set up with the purpose to collect spam. If spam appears with a certain number in theses spam traps, a unique signature is given and can be used to identify spam.

Trend Analysis: By analyzing the individual history of sent email by a user, resulting trends can help to improve the accuracy of spam detection and minimize occurrence of 'false-positive' mail.

4.1.2 New Approaches for encountering Spam

Reputation Networks: Reputation networks are generally based on White lists and filter systems based on social networks such as collaborative spam databases or Blacklists. Reputation networks take advantages of both techniques and extend them.[24]

All users connected to the network can assign "reputation" or "trust" scores to the people they know. The result is a large reputation data base which consists of the ratings of

---

[24] See GOLBECK AND HENDLER (2004), p. 1.

all connected users. Using all individual scores the system uses a recursive algorithm to infer a global reputation score for the sender of the message. The reputation score is displayed in the Inbox of the mail client next to the message. All messages can be sorted by value of the reputation score, making "good" messages more prominent.[25]

While the scoring system offers the same benefits as a White list, some of the problems are diminished. The content of the low priority folder is filtered with a higher accuracy, using the inferred ratings of the whole network. Even though there is still some burden on the user in setting up his reputation ratings, it is still possible to generally relay on the inferred network ratings.[26]

Due to the nature of the algorithm, Reputation networks are not intended to be a real solution to spam but as a technique to be combined with classical anti-spam filters to increase accuracy.

Challenge/Response System: The idea of a challenge/response system is to recognize if the sender of an email is human (unlike an email robot) and if the email is spam or relevant correspondence. The system works like an automatically generated White list by forcing the sender to verify that the email is relevant. Both robots and spammer are unlikely to respond the request.

The system keeps all incoming mail in a special folder and automatically generates an email which is send to the sender of the original mail. The system requests the sender to pass a "challenge", such as answering a question or recognizing a word in colored dots. These techniques are recently used to prevent robots from subscribing email accounts such as hotmail or yahoo. In case of a positive response, the mail is moved to the inbox and the sender can be placed on a White list.

Even though challenge/response systems have a very high accuracy in filtering spam, problems occur when legitimate email is send automatically by mail robots such as mailing lists or by CRM systems.

---

[25] See GOLBECK AND HENDLER (2004), p. 1.
[26] See GOLBECK AND HENDLER (2004), p. 1.

eStamps: The reason for the rise of spam is the fact that spam is free for the sender. This motivates the spammer to send almost unlimited amounts of spam. An economical solution would be to create a system which requires spammer to pay for their outgoing mail traffic.[27]

The eStamp model would oblige the senders of high amounts of email correspondence to buy eStamps for sending their correspondence. Regulations could make it possible for private users to use email for free due to the limited amount of email they send. The electronic stamp would be attached to the email and allow the user to send.[28]

The highest benefits from the system would be created for the ISPs. They suffer economically from the spam traffic as their infrastructure is being used and blocked. Electronic stamps enable them to generate new revenues by the selling of eStamps. Even the customer of the ISPs could benefit by a decreasing amount of spam and by sharing the ISPs stamp profits with them.[29]

The electronic stamp approach would require a lot of efforts in the beginning, but unlike other ways such as spam filters, not only the symptoms of spam would be battled but the problem would be addressed by the root. Electronic stamps could as well be more effective then legal solutions such as the CAN-SPAM Act, because history shows that economical sanctions are generally more effective then simply applying laws.[30]

4.2   Legislation

After years of relatively anarchic conditions in the internet, more and more people around the world agree on an urgent need for an obliging legal framework to encounter the spread of spam. The most serious attempt to control spam by legislation is the CAN-SPAM Act.

---

[27] See ARRISON (2004), p. 12.
[28] See ARRISON (2004), p. 13.
[29] See ARRISON (2004), p. 14.
[30] See ARRISON (2004), p. 15.

17

"The CAN-SPAM Act of 2003 (Public Law No. 108-187, was S.877 of the 108th Congress), signed into law by President Bush on December 16, 2003, establishes the United States' first national standards for the sending of commercial e-mail and requires the Federal Trade Commission (FTC) to enforce its provisions. The bill's full name is an acronym: Controlling the Assault of Non-Solicited Pornography and Marketing Act of 2003. Critics of the law's perceived weaknesses sometimes refer to it as You CAN SPAM."[31]

Unlike former US state laws which defined spam by the number of send items, by content or by the fact that it was unsolicited, the new CAN-SPAM Act defines spam as "any electronic mail message the primary purpose of which is the commercial advertisement or promotion of a commercial product or service (including content on an Internet website operated for a commercial purpose)."[32]

According to the CAN-SPAM Act sending spam can still be regarded as legal as long as certain requirements are fullfilled. The reciever has to have the possibility to sign out from the mailing list; a valid subject line and a correct header with complete routing information; a legitimate physical address of the sender; adult material has to be labeled explicitly.[33]

Problems in effectivly applying the new laws emerge from the fact, that tracing spam and spammers is relatively difficult. Due to the stabile but unsave and out dated SMTP protocoll for email applications it is easy for spammer to hide their real identy.[34]

"On February 1, 2005, a New York Times article suggested that the Can spam Act had resulted in little to no effect on the flow of spam, and the amount of spam saturating the Internet had actually increased since the law went into effect."[35]

---

[31] See WIKIPEDIA (2005).
[32] See LEGALARCHIVER (NO YEAR).
[33] See LEGALARCHIVER (NO YEAR).
[34] See BONEH (2004), p. 2.
[35] See WIKIPEDIA (2005).

18

5.   Concluding Remarks

Since the rise of the internet, email has brought along inevitable numerous blessings for the internet community, the globalization and the modern information society. But it is also an inevitable fact that recently the exponential growth of the global email traffic has led to significant damage for ISPs, the user community, the economy and public. And the trend is sustainable going up.

To cope with the new problems and to find back to an efficient and pleasant use of email, not only symptoms but also the roots for the trend should be addressed. On the side of the relevant correspondence, integrated solutions such as email Lifecycle Management, new approaches for email clients such as "IBM – reinventing email" and also concepts such as Semantic email[36] are promising.

On the side of spam, no single approach can solve the problem by its own. An intelligent mixture of all relevant methods such as spam filtering together with an effective legal framework, changes in the basic email technology through new and up to date transfer protocols and explicit signatures for identification but also a change in the personal behavior of the users concerning internet and email must go hand in hand.

---

[36] See MCDOWELL, ETZIONI, HALEVY AND LEVY (2004), p. 1.

19

References

ARRISON, SONJA (2004): *Pacific Research Institute - Canning spam: An Economic Solution To Unwanted email*, San Francisco, retrieved on September 15, 2005 from http:// www.pacificresearch.org/ pub/sab/techno/2004/spam01-26-04.pdf

BLACKSPIDER TECHNOLOGIES (2004): *Spam Datasheet – Mailcontrol Spam Technology Overview*, retrieved on September 15, 2005 from http://www.blackspider.com/news_ and_resources/spam_datasheet.pdf

BONEH, DAN (2004): *The Difficulties of Tracing Spam Email*, Department of Computer Science, Stanford University, retrieved on September 15, 2005 from http://www.ftc.gov/reports/rewardsys/expertrpt_boneh.pdf

DAWSON, RAY / JACKSON, THOMAS / WILSON, DARREN (NO YEAR): *The Cost of email Interruption*, Computer Science Department, Loughborough University, Loughborough, retrieved on September 15, 2005 from http://interruptions.net/literature/Jackson-JOSIT-01.pdf

DOUBLECLICK (2004): *Doubleclick Inc. - Consumer Email Study*, retrieved on September 15, 2005 from http:// www.doubleclick.com/us/knowledge_central/ documents/ RESEARCH/dc_consumer_email_0410.pdf

EPRIVACY GROUP (2003): S*pam By Numbers*, retrieved on September 15, 2005 from http://blog.cauce.ca/blog/archives/spamByNumbers.pdf

FELLOWS, DEBORAH (2003): *Pew Internet & American Life Project – How It Is Hurting Email And Degrading Life On The Internet*, Washington, retrieved on September 15, 2005 from http:// www.pewinternet.org/pdfs/PIP_spam_Report.pdf

20

FORRESTER RESEARCH (2002) in RIEGER, GÖTZ / SCHAPIRO, SCHLOMO (2004): *Die Bedeutung von email: gestern – heute – morgen*, p. 8, retrieved on September 15, 2005 from http://www.probusiness.de/aktuelles/ documents/email_Historie.pdf

GOLBECK , JENNIFER / HENDLER, JAMES (2004): *Reputation Network Analysis For email Filtering, University of Maryland,* retrieved on September 15, 2005 from http:// www.ceas.cc/papers-2004/177.pdf

GROUP TECHNOLOGIES (2005): *GROUP Technologies AG - E-Mail Lifecycle Mangement - Strategien für Verarbeitung, Ablage, Sicherung und Integration von E-Mail in die wichtigsten Geschäftsanwendungen und Prozesse,* Karlsruhe, retrieved on September 15, 2005 from http://www.group-technologies.com/share/pdf/products/white_paper/ ELM-whitepaper_de.pdf

IBM (2003): *IBM – Remail – Reinventing Email,* retrieved on September 15, 2005 from http://www.research.ibm.com/remail/threads.html

IDC (NO YEAR) in RIEGER, GÖTZ / SCHAPIRO, SCHLOMO (2004): *Die Bedeutung von email: gestern – heute – morgen,* p. 6, retrieved on September 15, 2005 from http://www.probusiness.de/aktuelles/ documents/email_Historie.pdf

LEGALARCHIVER (NO YEAR): *CAN-SPAM Act 2003,* retrieved on September 15, 2005 from http://www.legalarchiver.org/cs.htm

MCDOWELL, LUKE / ETZIONI, OREN / HALEVY, ALON / LEVY, HENRY (2004): *Semantic Email,* Department of Computer Science and Engineering, University of Washington, retrieved on September 15, 2005 from http:// www.cs.washington.edu/research/semweb/pubs/www2004.pdf

RIEGER, GÖTZ / SCHAPIRO, SCHLOMO (2004): *Pro Business AG - Die Bedeutung von email: gestern – heute – morgen,* retrieved on September 15, 2005 from http://www.probusiness.de/aktuelles/ documents/email_Historie.pdf

21

STEIN, MICHAEL (2004): *Get Active Software – Put email to Work – Without Becoming a spam Artist,* retrieved on September 15, 2005 from
http://www.getactive.com/pdf/ white-papers/put_email_to_work.pdf

WHITTAKER, STEVE / JONES, QUENTIN / TERVEEN1, LOREN (2002): *Managing long term communications: Conversation and Contact Management, AT&T Labs Research, New Jersey Institute of Technology,* New Jersey, retrieved on September 15, 2005 from
http://csdl.computer.org/comp/proceedings/ hicss/2002/1435/04/14350115b.pdf

WHITTAKER, STEVE / SIDNER, CANDACE (1996): *Lotus Development Corporation - email overload: exploring personal information management of ernail,* Cambridge, re-trieved on September 15, 2005 from
http://www.clarkson.edu/~clarkbw/hci/papers/p276-whittaker.pdf

WIKIPEDIA (2005): *CAN-SPAM Act of 2005,* retrieved on September 15, 2005 from
http://en.wikipedia.org/wiki/Can_Spam_Act_of_2003

YAHOO (2005): *Yahoo Directory,* retrieved on September 15, 2005 from
http://dir.yahoo.com/Business_and_Economy/Business_to_Business/Computers/Comm unications_and_Networking/Software/email/Junk_email_Removal_and_Filtering/